Caring for
Books and Documents

Illis quos dilexi quattuor

Caring for
Books and Documents

2nd edition

A. D. BAYNES-COPE

With line illustrations by Sture Åkerström

Published in association with
The British Library

NEW AMSTERDAM
New York

Acknowledgements

I am grateful to a large number of people who have helped, directly and indirectly, in the production of this booklet. Many people, during my career in the Scientific Civil Service, have taught me about paper, books, archives and libraries, care and climates. From my mother I learned the importance of proper ventilation and building maintenance. Other colleagues, notably Mrs Felicity Strong and Dr Ulla Ehrensvärd, read and corrected the text. I am also grateful to Dr Dennis Allsopp of the CAB International Mycological Institute for much help over many years. Mrs C. M. Phillips, of Southampton University Library advised on the section on Electronic Records.

The greatest thanks are due to the kind friend and master bookbinder who provided the superb line drawings in the margins, Sture Åkerström.

First Published 1981 by British Museum Publications

First published in the United States of America in 1989 by
NEW AMSTERDAM BOOKS
171 Madison Avenue
New York, NY 10016
By arrangement with The British Library, London

Printed in England

Contents

Introduction

Many people have collections of books, or volunteer to look after books in small libraries, or are required as a part of their business to look after documents (as in a solicitor's office), and sooner or later a situation will occur in which the owner or custodian will feel the need for practical advice. For many years, the Research Laboratory of the British Museum has received requests for advice from people who have problems with books and documents and, though these requests are now transferred to the British Library, it seemed that a small booklet based on this Laboratory's accumulated experience would be welcome.

It is essentially a book of advice and guidance rather than a set of instructions because our experience has been that, while some enquiries could be met with a simple answer, many could be answered only by trying to find a compromise between what was needed by the books and what the owner could afford by way of space, conditions, skill, time and money. It was exceptional for the books themselves, much less the premises, to be seen by the member of staff trying to answer the enquiry and the usual procedure has been to give a brief account of what was required with an explanation of why it was needed, so that the owner could work out his own compromises. This has been made much easier by the present determination to Do-It-Yourself.

This booklet contains a great deal of 'Why' and what may seem to be too little 'How', but this is believed to be the best way to help the owners and custodians of libraries to solve their own variations on a common problem; for this, as Maimonides said, was the best form of assistance. Those who wish can go straight to the section on What to Do, but it has been the author's hope in writing this booklet that the very brief accounts of the materials of which books and documents are made, and of their enemies, will whet the reader's appetite to learn more of the subject.

A rather broadly-based bibliography has been added. Apart from matters concerning the storage of books and documents, about which there is little published to help the man in the street, there are books on repairs and bindings, topics which are not covered in this booklet but about which the owner or custodian will obviously need to know. He is warned that such work needs a fairly high level of manual dexterity and skill, if it is to be done at all. Other books, if not immediately relevant to storage, are added as sources of useful information on problems that may arise.

A. D. BAYNES-COPE, Research Laboratory, British Museum

Introduction to the Second Edition

The main differences in this edition are in the amplification of the section on relative humidity, and in the much-expanded 'Bookshelf', which still lists the author's own collection. There are also three new appendices: one gives brief guidance on the storage of electronic data, following the inclusion of this matter in the revised edition of BS 5454. The other two depart from the author's official work, being an account of how a 'Do-It-Yourself' man did it himself, making his own library stacks for his books and organising his collection.

A. D. BAYNES-COPE, Stanton, Suffolk, 1989

Helping a man to help himself.

Air conditioning is a fairly recent development.

1

Theoretical aspects of care

Ideal conditions

It is well to begin with a consideration of what experts believe to be the best conditions for the storage of books and documents. Two factors are involved, temperature and relative humidity, and this latter term must be explained. Save in exceptional circumstances, air always contains some moisture and the amount that it can hold is related to the temperature: the higher the temperature of air, the greater its capacity to hold moisture but it rarely contains the maximum possible amount. The relative humidity is quite simply the ratio of what is actually present to the maximum possible – at the same temperature – and for convenience it is expressed as a percentage. It follows that if the temperature of a closed volume of air is altered, when the air is heated, the relative humidity goes down and when it is cooled, the relative humidity goes up. If that air is cooled to the temperature at which its relative humidity reaches 100 per cent, or saturation, dew begins to form, so that temperature is called the Dew Point. A mist is quite simply air which is saturated with moisture and has an excess in the form of tiny droplets. If in an air space there is a cold place, the air round it can become saturated and condensation occurs, as is seen on cold windows. It must be remembered that condensation does not occur on windows alone but also on cold walls, ceilings, floors, shelving, especially metal, and even books if they are brought from a very cold place to a warm one.

In the United Kingdom, which by world standards has an equable climate, the proper conditions for the storage of books and documents (indeed, many other things such as wood), are regarded as being at a steady point between 55°F (13°C) and 65°F (18°C) with the relative humidity at a steady point between 50 and 65 per cent. It has to be said that experts from countries in different climatic zones often prefer to vary these conditions somewhat, and there are sensible reasons for this. The United Kingdom is regarded as having large amounts of books and documents on parchment or vellum which reacts more strongly towards changes in relative humidity than does paper and it is considered wise to let it remain a little more flexible. It is also necessary to take into account the changes that occur when a book is brought from a conditioned store to a reading room at the local ambient level of temperature and humidity. The conditions for human comfort are warmer than those desirable for books and a person sitting still soon becomes cold. It has to be understood that, apart from its leaves, a book has a mechanical structure

9

which has built into it a very subtle balance of forces and the composite nature of this structure, involving often wood, cardboard, leather, parchment, paper, cloth and adhesives makes it, also, sensitive to climatic changes, as anyone who has read a book by the fire on a cold day and noticed a curl form in the covers will realise.

Air-conditioning is a fairly recent development of the last 50 years or so and all libraries contain books bound long before it was invented. For hundreds of years books have been bound, stored and read in conditions which are far from those now regarded as ideal and it is easy to show that books can be safe in temperatures far below 55°F (13°C). Mediæval monasteries must have been very cold in winter and the monks' habits were thick and warm.

For most people, in ordinary circumstances, the theoretically ideal conditions are not attainable, for to achieve them a system of much complexity is required, using trunking to deliver conditioned, clean, filtered air in adequate amounts; few can afford this or can accommodate the size of equipment needed. Furthermore, as librarians, archivists and conservators know all too well, much time and trouble is needed to adjust the system after it has been installed. It must be monitored by reliable instruments, continuously, and there must be ready access to some means of expert assistance if it malfunctions. It is now realised, too, that biological problems are added to engineering ones, and in fact, over the last two decades there has been a move towards reducing, by careful design and construction, the extent to which air-conditioning has to be used in new libraries and archives.

On the other hand, provided that we know what books and documents are made of, and how these materials can be expected to behave in various climatic conditions, what their enemies are and how to outwit them, and what can help a room to keep a steady climate (or at least have only gentle fluctuations in the climate), we shall be able to bring this knowledge together to produce conditions in which books and documents can be kept safely with a minimum of cost.

Time, thought, trouble and money must be expended, but not necessarily to an extent excessive in proportion to the value of a collection. Thoughtless neglect can easily result in the ruin of important, beautiful, interesting or treasured books and documents.

The materials of books and documents

It is necessary to understand what books and documents are made of if the best storage conditions are to be chosen for them. Since about the beginning of the Christian era, papyrus has declined in importance, while two materials, parchment and paper (traditionally said to have been invented at about the same time in two different lands, Asia Minor and China), have completely supplanted it.

Parchment is said to take its name from the old city of Pergamum and both parchment and vellum are made from the skins of animals. Vellum is supposed to be made from the whole skin of the calf and parchment from the split-off skins of lambs and goats. Other animals' skins may be used, such as deer, and the Royal Library in Stockholm owns what is believed to be the world's largest manuscript, written on donkey skin.

The skin taken from the animal is treated with lime to remove hair, the wet skin is stretched on a frame and then repeatedly damped, scraped and dried until it is smooth and even in thickness. The method of manufacture, coupled with the fact that an animal's skin is not naturally flat, results in the prepared skin being under severe strain and the stress produced can be released when it is repeatedly exposed to extremes of temperature and humidity.

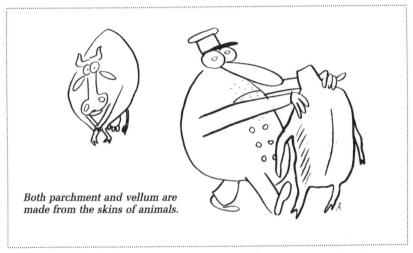

Both parchment and vellum are made from the skins of animals.

According to tradition, paper was invented by Tsai Lun, Chief Eunuch to the Emperor of China, in AD 106 but there is reason to believe that a form of paper was in existence many years before then. The knowledge of papermaking spread westward, reaching Christian Europe in the 13th century.

The essential ingredient of paper is cellulose fibre, though in recent years mineral and synthetic fibres have been used for special purposes and silk and hair have been incorporated in security documents. Cellulose is one of nature's most important building materials and it supplies the support for all plants, from grasses to trees. Until the middle of the 19th century the only fibre source for western paper was cotton and linen rags, the long, strong linen fibres from flax making the most superior paper. In brief, the rags were cleaned, sometimes bleached by the sun and finally broken down in a stamping mill until a slurry of small fibres was obtained. The Dutch invention of the beater or 'Hollander' during the 17th century produced fibres with more splaying out (fibrillation), but the most important development was the invention of the paper-making machine in 1812, which could produce paper at a rate greater than any vatman (who made four or five sheets a minute). The machine needed fibre in quantities that the conversion of old rags alone could not provide and this led to the introduction of fibres made from grasses and wood. A temporary expedient, still in use today, was the addition of mineral diluents such as china clay or chalk to the paper fibre, and it is now known that the addition of chalk (calcium carbonate) to paper is chemically advantageous. However, very often in the 1820s–1830s, excessive quantities of loading were added in paper-making, so that there were many complaints of newish paper breaking up into dust. A more undesirable diluent for the fibres is finely ground wood, called in England 'mechanical wood-pulp', though the American term 'ground-wood' is more descriptive. This material adds no strength to paper and since it absorbs and retains acid gases from the atmosphere, as well as darkening on exposure to light and air, its presence is positively detrimental to paper, making it weak and brittle.

Cellulose fibres alone, cast into the form of a sheet, cannot provide a suitable writing material, for this would produce blotting or filter paper, which is too absorbent, and not writing paper; but when the cotton fibres are coated and consolidated with glue size we have a usable writing paper. Glue is the traditional size, often made by boiling down scrap parchment; this leaves the paper more flexible than when glue from boiled bones is used. Aluminium sulphate, or 'papermakers' alum', when added to glue causes the solution to become thicker so that the sizing process can be more effective, but this results in a very undesirable increase in acidity.

Hand-made paper was sized after, not during, manufacture, and the inconvenience of this extra process was even more apparent with machine manufacture, so a new method of sizing, 'engine-sizing', was developed in which the sizing occurred during the formation of the paper. This method used a mixture of alum and resin, but, as with alum-glue sizes, caused an undesirable increase in the acidity of the paper. Within the last few years neutral sizes for papers have been developed, though they are not as yet widely used.

A little about cellulose

Cellulose itself is a polymer; that is, it forms a large molecule composed of a great number of smaller identical units. The unit in the case of cellulose is a sugar called cellobiose, which is itself made up of two molecules of glucose. The cellulose molecule forms a single long unbranched chain, and bundles of these molecules lie side by side to form sub-units which in turn build up the fibre. (This is an over-simplified description, but it will serve our purpose.)

The glucose molecule contains six carbon atoms in a chain; each carbon atom has oxygen and hydrogen atoms attached to it. Five of the carbon atoms and one oxygen atom form a ring which has on its periphery oxygen atoms linked to hydrogen atoms, which the chemist calls hydroxyl groups, so that all the way along the cellulose molecule there are hydroxyl groups projecting from the long chains of rings. What is so important in the use of cellulose for making paper is that water molecules can form a semi-chemical bond to these hydroxyl groups and thus forcing the long chains apart. Normally, 'dry' cellulose may contain seven per cent of water, and if the cellulose fibre is dehydrated drastically the fibre will shrink widthways and even suffer damage. When the fibres are well soaked in water they expand widthways but not lengthways, becoming very soft and flexible. Under ordinary conditions the amount of water retained in the fibre is dependent on the relative humidity of the atmosphere surrounding it, so that it gains or loses water as this varies.

This has important consequences. The wet relaxed cellulose fibres can felt together to form, when dried out, a tough cohesive sheet, and this sheet will vary in area according to the residual moisture content of the fibres. Hand-made paper will expand very nearly equally along the length or breadth of the sheet, while machine-made paper will expand or contract almost entirely across the direction in which the paper moves through the machine because the fibres tend to align in the machine direction. This alignment also affects the ease with which paper can be torn or folded.

Parchment and vellum

Parchment and vellum are made of a protein called collagen and this, like all proteins, is composed of a number of different amino acids united together to form chains. Though the chemical composition of collagen is completely different from that of cellulose and its physical structure is a natural mesh of interlocking fibres, collagen reacts towards moisture in a way similar to that of cellulose. However, the extent of movement is greater and the great strength of the sheet means that the stresses induced by the movements can be greater, particularly if the skin is dried excessively. There is a further chemical difference to be considered. The long chains making up the cellulose molecules are liable to be broken down by acids, more so than the collagen molecules, since paper can have been made with an acid size, whereas parchment has chalk, an alkali, in it. Paper has in many, but not all, circumstances a lower durability than parchment and this is particularly noticeable in city atmospheres. Against this, paper can withstand wetting and flood conditions far better than parchment and, within limits, both excessive drying and heat are less damaging to paper than to parchment.

Art paper

For certain purposes, particularly for fine art printing and illustration, a special type of paper called 'art paper' was developed, and this has a smooth, glossy, heavily loaded surface. It usually has a binder in the surface which is badly affected by water, but in recent years art paper less susceptible to damage by water has been developed. It is usual for the inner fibrous core of art paper to be of poor quality. It is not unusual for the leaves of a book printed on art paper to stick together if they become damp, and severe damage can occur when an attempt is made to open the book.

Inks

For a sheet of writing material, parchment, vellum or paper (either a single sheet or bound in a book) to become a document, it must be written or printed on. The earliest of inks may have been coloured plant juices. The ancient Egyptians used a mixture of soot and gum for writing on papyrus or pot-sherds, but this is not a good ink for writing on parchment, which is rather greasy and impervious. At about the beginning of the Christian era, it was discovered that by mixing an aqueous extract of oak galls with a solution of ferrous sulphate, a deep blue-black colour was obtained, and if gum arabic was added to the solution an excellent writing ink was produced.

This ink, nowadays called iron gallotannate ink, has proved to be one of the most durable of all inks, but if badly made it can be so acid as to damage both paper and parchment, and when exposed to excessively powerful light it can fade badly although not irrecoverably. The development of synthetic organic dye-stuffs has allowed the introduction of brightly coloured writing inks which are more likely than not to fade.

Printing ink has until very recent years been made from carbon black and oil, and such an ink cannot fade. However, some printing inks used today are based on synthetic dyes which can fade.

Bindings

The materials of books and the methods in which they are used have varied over the centuries. The original form of a very large document was a long roll of papyrus, and in every synagogue today the Scrolls of the Law are written on sheets of parchment sewn edge to edge to form a long roll wound onto two wooden 'Trees of Life'.

The first books that were in the form with which we are familiar were made in the Middle East in the early centuries of the Christian era. Gradually, the practice of gathering groups of folded sheets, and sewing them onto cords or thongs which were then laced into wooden boards (these boards then being covered with leather), was developed into the system for binding books which is still used today. Parchment or vellum may be used instead of leather and alum–tawed or 'whittawed' skin, especially pig skin, has been used for many centuries to cover books.

For many purposes 'boards' made from compressed paper pulp have replaced wooden boards, and since early in the 19th century cloth in various forms (especially buckram, which is a coated cloth) has replaced leather. A more important change has been the development of 'casing' to replace binding. In casing, the boards are already covered before they are applied to the book (which is usually sewn by machinery) and fastened by adhesives.

One early method of binding which was popular for several centuries was the 'limp vellum' cover. This is simply a sheet of vellum folded round the sewn sections, with the vellum thongs onto which the sections were sewn laced into the cover. The edges of the cover were folded in and the inner surfaces covered with the end papers. It was a quick, simple and cheap method of binding but, unlike true binding in boards, it gives no real support to the leaves and such books require an external support if they are not to sag and become distorted on the shelves.

The modern paperback is a development of the appallingly misnamed 'perfect' binding introduced in the 19th century. The pages are not parts of folded gatherings but are individual leaves and are fastened to each other and the cover by an adhesive, originally gutta percha, worked into the edge. Bitter experience, both with perfect bindings and paperbacks, has shown that neither can be relied on for durability, though some of the more expensive paperbacks are made in sewn sections from excellent paper.

2

The enemies of books and documents

Having described, rather briefly, the materials of which books and documents are made and how they are put together, it is necessary to consider those factors – chemical, physical, mechanical and biological – which act against them, and which we can describe as the enemies of books and documents. Indeed, the enemies may be internal and almost inseparable from a book in the sense that poor materials and poor construction are both major causes of deterioration, so we can include human beings as an enemy of books through sins of omission and commission in the creation, use and care of them.

The division of the enemies of books and documents into exact classes is troublesome. Light, micro-organisms, acids and pollution are in reality only four varieties of chemical attack. The teeth of mice, woodworms and projecting nails act mechanically, and heat acts both chemically and mechanically. A 'bad climate' for the storage of books can mean that it is correct in respect of temperature and humidity but that it is grossly polluted by acid fumes. However, it is convenient to consider the enemies of books and documents by simple, arbitrary classes.

Physical and mechanical damage

This happens to a book whenever it is ill-treated. It can occur when a book is dropped, scraped against another, against the bottom of the shelf above, against projecting nails etc., or when a book projecting from a shelf is knocked by someone passing by. It can also be caused when a book is not supported properly, even if it is never moved. A floppy or weak book will twist and sag if it is not supported adequately along the whole of its bottom edge and on both sides; this is a common fault when a thick book is cased rather than made into a proper binding, whether the sections are sewn or not, for the text drops at the foredge.

Physical damage can also be caused by excessive drying, which in practice is usually the result of excessive heat. Parchment will cockle badly when it is too dry and the covers of books can be badly distorted. Book covers are almost invariably made of three layers: the outer cover, the board and the lining or endpaper; the bookbinder should choose all three so that when assembled with the direction of the paper lying correctly, small and gentle movements in any one layer are compensated by counter movements of the others, but this can only occur when the changes in humidity are neither too great nor too rapid. Most people have noticed the curve which develops on the cover of a book when it is being read on the lap close to a fire, but the same effect can be caused when a book is kept in any very hot place and it is not unknown for the board to warp so much that the cover may be ripped away at the head and tail of the hinge. However, provided that real damage has not been done, the cover will regain its normal flatness when it is returned to a less dry place.

Of all the forms of damage, physical damage is the one most easily prevented by simple care. Very large books should be laid flat on their sides and no book should be placed on a shelf so that it projects beyond the shelf. It is best to keep one shelf, or even one stack, deeper and with more height between shelves than the others, for large books. Extra care should be taken with the books at the ends of shelves, and if necessary a piece of wood or hardboard should be placed against the sides or ends of the case to prevent nails, bolts or other fittings from touching the covers of the books. It is also important that a book should glide easily off the shelf when it is withdrawn. When steel racking is used, the angle iron forming the upright corners of the stack will often prevent the end books from coming straight out; extra packing may be useful here to avoid bending and straining the book.

Books should never be packed tightly on a shelf and books which are greatly different in height should not be placed side by side. They should be packed just firmly enough to support each other but not so tight that they jam when an attempt is made to withdraw them. If very dry books are placed in an environment rather more humid than that in which they have hitherto been kept, they will swell, and in these circumstances it is wise to leave them a little loose at first. Though the headband of a properly bound book is designed to ensure its safety when it is withdrawn by pulling from the top, in a cased book the headband is partly ornamental. In either case it is best to avoid any risk by withdrawing a book from a shelf by grasping the centre of the spine.

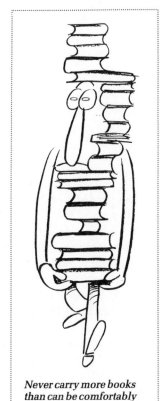

Never carry more books than can be comfortably held in one hand.

As books can so easily be damaged by being dropped, even onto a soft carpet, it is wise never to carry more books than can comfortably be held in one hand, but to use a shopping bag. Baskets should be used only if there are no projecting ends of withies, unless they have a padded lining. If many books or bundles of documents have to be moved often, a proper trolley should be used and small strong tables placed strategically

17

around the room are a help. Remember, too, that when moving books, it is necessary to open doors, pass through them and close them again, and it is very easy to drop a pile of books while fumbling with a door handle. The essence of good care is that it is never dodged or diminished for convenience's sake.

A modern source of damage to books arises from photocopying, when books are opened as wide as possible and pressed down by brute force onto the platen. This will almost invariably cause strain and damage to the binding structure on the first occasion and when it is repeated the damage becomes rapidly worse. No book should be treated in this way and books should only be photocopied if they open flat *easily*.

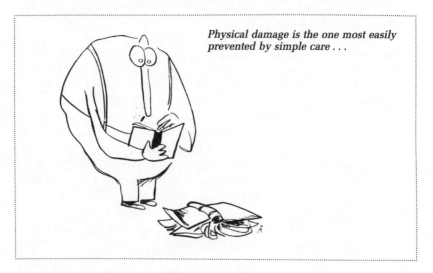

Physical damage is the one most easily prevented by simple care . . .

Biological enemies

These can be divided into three groups: Animals, Insects and Micro-organisms. The problems of damage caused by living organisms, that is, biodeterioration, may be understood better by thinking first about living organisms in general. All of them, including man, have certain needs. These are, briefly, the right climate of temperature and humidity; an environment which is not hazardous to life; and the right food, which includes not only the major items, such as protein, carbohydrate and fat, but minor constituents such as minerals and vitamins, to an extent which depends on the nature of the organism. There can also be a need for what might loosely be called 'shelter', and for a source of energy. Given the right climate, any organism thrives best on its own proper, balanced diet in an adequate amount. If the balance is wrong, if any part of the diet is wholly or partially lacking, the organism will not thrive to its maximum extent; it will be smaller, develop more slowly and be less likely to multiply. A really rampant infestation requires optimum conditions, but even in relatively poor conditions, growth will occur and will be damaging to the books and documents which we wish to preserve in a handsome state. There is no sharp demarcation between the conditions the organism needs for lush growth and those in which it cannot grow; and it will grow if it can.

The materials of which books and documents are made are foodstuffs for many living creatures, not necessarily ideal, though all too often good enough. It should be realised too that even if the proper materials of books are not always an optimum balanced diet for deleterious organisms, the presence of dirt, especially heavy finger-marking, may provide the extras which can make them more desirable. Finger dirt is hygroscopic and the ease with which it absorbs moisture from the atmosphere may make it the first point of attack by microbes. The building and its contents may be shelter for part of a life-cycle of an organism. (An example of this latter is a spider's cocoon. Spiders eat only insects, but the cocoon is a messy nuisance.) It is important, therefore, if evidence of any infestation is found, to make some attempt to identify it and to learn its habits, in order to mount an effective attack on it. This does not apply strictly to fungal infestation, for the identification of fungi may be very difficult, even for experts, and in this case it is better to use a 'general' method of attack, such as lowering humidity levels.

In all cases, elimination of the infestation is only part of the problem – the factors leading to it must be eliminated too, and subsequent cleaning of affected material may require expert assistance in forms which are outside the scope of this book.

Animals

Animals can damage books and documents by simple mechanical destruction, as when mice tear up paper for nest-making, or by fouling as when bats, birds, cats or mice deposit excrement or fleas. It is not difficult to design a building, or protect a part of it, so that unwanted access by animals is impossible, though bats and mice can find their way through remarkably small holes.

Where there is a risk that birds may enter down chimneys or through open doors or broken windows, the open spaces can be covered by wire mesh. Neither chimneys, fireplaces nor ventilators should be blocked up unless for some extraordinary reason this is absolutely unavoidable; instead, strong wire grids should be used to cover them so as not to interfere with air movement.

However, if birds are not a direct problem unless they actually enter a book store (when their excrement is remarkably damaging, for it is chemically highly reactive) they can present an indirect problem. Their nests are filthy and provide a rich food source for many insects that can attack books, as can the dead bodies of fledglings and mature birds. Thus, birds in a roof, or in any space connecting with a book store, are a potent source of infestations and they must be eliminated. A good builder may

. . . bats, birds, cats and mice deposit excrement and fleas . . .

often provide the first and best defence against some insect infestations.

Where there is a large population of feral or semi-feral cats in or around a building, care must be taken to ensure that they do not enter the book or document store. The removal of an enraged and frightened cat is not easy, and the smell and mess it leaves behind is difficult to clean up. What may not be realised is that such cats carry fleas and these release eggs which can remain fertile for long periods. The eggs are sensitive to vibration and even footfalls can make them hatch remarkably quickly, for they mean that food, and life, is at hand.

It is not generally realised, except by those who have suffered the misery of a flea infestation, that fleas, which do not attack books, are as troublesome to eliminate as insects which do. A remarkably high proportion of flea infestations, both of dwellings and work places, are of cat fleas rather than the human variety.

Mice and bats can enter a room through quite small holes. Bats can crawl through a hole the size of a man's thumb-nail, and in old buildings – in the roofs, walls and wainscoatings – there will be plenty of these. Such holes must be found and blocked; where wire screens are used to cover holes, the mesh must be ¼ in (6 mm) or less as baby mice which are old enough to live independently can crawl through holes which are only slightly larger than this. Further, like those of birds, the nests of rats and mice, and their dead bodies, are foci for insect infestations.

It is said that there has been some success with the electronic devices and with chemicals which bats loathe but there appears to be no certain simple cheap remedy. If the book and document store is only a store and not, for example, an elegant library visited for its appearance, extensive wire mesh screens can be used. Recent legislation has made the prevention of damage from bats much less easy.

For the elimination of bats and mice, it is generally advisable to consult a reputable firm with experience backed by laboratory facilities. The poison baits which may be used would probably not be harmful to books and documents but there is a general rule, which should always be observed, that materials must never be added to documents without real need, and the contamination of books by toxic materials is unforgivable.

One final precaution that is often forgotten is that food should never be left or eaten in a book or document store, for any crumbs or residues are an open invitation to pests.

Insects

The enemies of books and documents described under this heading are, in many cases, not what the entomologist would classify as insects. The range of small pests that damage them is too wide for the use of exact definitions to be helpful in a small book and, rightly or wrongly, the term 'insect' is used here for simplicity. Books and documents in a library, living-room or store can offer a living to many kinds of insects. Some will do no more than graze on moulds, others will live on the wood of shelves, spiders will eat only other insects thereby making unsightly webs, but there are insects which will eat the components of books, paper, parchment, leather, paste and glue, while some will burrow deeply into a book to pupate.

Generally speaking, wood-boring insects appear to live indifferently in wood or book, but it may be that some components of the wood other than the cellulose or lignin are desirable to them. It is common to find that larvae have moved through a book in such a way as to suggest that they were merely on passage. Firebrats and silver-fish will eat paper if it is to their liking, and it is not unusual to find that modern chemical wood-pulp has been attacked by these creatures in preference to sound 18th-century rag paper. They will also eat the paste filling of buckram, leaving the cotton or linen thread unattacked. The rather patchy loss of colour gives at first sight the impression that extensive white mould is present but on closer examination the difference is clear.

The 'book louse', *Psocoptera,* is merely a browser on mould (which

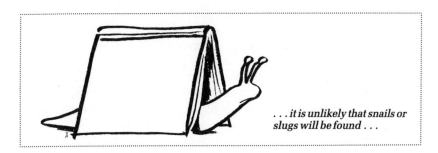

. . . it is unlikely that snails or slugs will be found . . .

should not be present anyway) and serves as a useful warning that storage conditions are poor, either by being seen or, quite often, by producing unpleasant casts which affect the eyes and noses of readers.

Dermestids are the most notable example of insects which move into a building by way of a primary infestation in the nests of birds, mice and rats, and their dead bodies. The larvae of Dermestids (for example the Hide or Bacon Beetles) feed on protein and will eat parchment or leather, but they may do even more damage by burrowing deeply into books to make safe haven for their pupation.

It is unlikely that snails or slugs will be found in book or document stores unless truly appalling conditions of damp and neglect exist, but it is worth mentioning that both can digest cellulose and are known to cause damage to letters in post-boxes.

Since most insects are highly mobile, it is probable that there is no practical way of excluding them totally from a store or library but there is no doubt that good housekeeping is of outstanding importance in denying them the chance to become a major infestation.

Most insects are highly mobile . . .

Almost the first requirement for a library, or a book and document store, is that every part of it – ceiling, walls, floor and fittings – is readily accessible for thorough and determined cleaning if an infestation occurs. Insecticides should be regarded as a last resort when the unexpected has happened in a well-cared-for store. The leading United Kingdom expert on insect infestations has stated flatly that rugs and carpets have no place in a library or book store: this may be harsh, but it is true. Apart from being shelter, especially for flea eggs, insects which eat woollen materials can and do eat protein materials in books.

When an insect 'infestation' does occur, it will be either in a book (or documents loose in a box) or in a fitting, under or in a floor covering, perhaps in all of them and the remedial treatment must be extended to both the fittings and the books and documents in *and around* the site of the infestation. The treatment must be designed to cope as far as is possible with the likelihood that all four stages of insect growth – egg, larva, pupa and insect – are present.

The first step in dealing with an infestation is to clear and clean the affected area; even if only one book is affected, those books on that shelf, and the ones above, below and backing onto it, must be examined thoroughly, preferably out of doors, and the infected books brushed with a soft paint-brush or gently with a vacuum cleaner fitted with a softish baluster brush. The shelves and uprights must be checked meticulously for worm-holes and frass if wood-worm is likely, for silver-fish, firebrats and book lice. If silver-fish or firebrats are suspected, the floor coverings also must be removed, particularly if there is a warm area from a fire-place, heating pipes or radiators, for these creatures will often live under linoleum and emerge at night to feed, perhaps travelling many feet through gaps in walls below floor level.

It is possible to fumigate books, provided that they are not too large. The book should be stood up opened fanwise in a container which can be closed and sealed together with a small jar holding chloroform at the rate of half a fluid ounce (about 15 ml) per cubic yard or cubic metre of space. The container is sealed and left for ten days. It must be opened out of doors. It is possible to treat quite large books in the same way in a large polythene 'blanket tidy' or dustbin liner placed round a cardboard box which provides the necessary rigidity. After fumigation, the book should be kept apart in case eggs or pupae have not been killed and develop later.

This method of fumigation is reasonably effective, but where books have very thick covers into which wood-worms have bored deeply, it cannot be expected to be as effective as fumigation in a vacuum chamber with a highly insecticidal gas. In such cases, or where very large books or many books are affected, the owner or custodian must give serious thought to employing a reputable firm who have the equipment and the expertise required to use a gas such as ethylene oxide or methyl bromide. The local museum or record office will generally know of such firms in their region.

In recent years, intense cold has been used as a safe means of killing insects in sensitive materials. Since the success of the method depends to a great extent on very rapid cooling to a very low temperature, (as low as $-40°F/C$) this temperature being reached throughout the volume, its use should be left to those experts who have equipment capable of doing this, for it is essential that the very resistant eggs and pupae are killed. A domestic deep-freeze is not adequate, but it is very useful for the temporary storage of infected material, in effect, for buying time.

Any book found to be infested with insects should be taken out of doors and cleaned thoroughly with a soft brush. A vacuum cleaner, even with a soft baluster brush, is a little fierce but the suck can be reduced by drilling a few ¼in or ⅜in (6mm or 9mm) holes in the tubing. Once the book is clean, it should be wrapped in a good polythene bag to prevent it from drying out in storage and treatment.

The fittings, shelves, and so on must also be cleaned thoroughly and it is advisable to treat them with a reputable proprietary insecticide fluid if any worm-holes are detected, but great care must be taken to ensure that they are thoroughly dried before re-use and that there are no residues left where they can affect the book. It is helpful, however, to have such material in cracks and crevices where insects may lurk so that they cannot act as foci of future infestations. Every detected worm-hole can be filled with a tiny blob of wax, pressed in with the finger, after treatment has been completed, as this makes it easier to spot new holes.

Where there is an infestation of firebrats or silver-fish, the area in which they congregate must be found and cleared out. If it is under linoleum or around heating pipes, it is advisable to treat the area with dusting powder containing a stable contact insecticide (such as DDT or BHC). It may even be necessary to fumigate the underfloor space with an insecticide smoke.

It is difficult to form a certain opinion on the use of insecticidal strips, which contain and give off DDVP (Dichlorvos). This insecticide is very effective but many people regard it as being undesirably toxic and there is no information available on the effect of the residues on books. Nevertheless, where a room must be left untended for prolonged periods, it offers very considerable advantages in providing a powerful protection against flying insects of all kinds.

Micro-organisms (microbes)

The term 'micro-organisms' is used in this section to describe moulds, fungi, bacteria, etc. which can live on, disfigure or destroy the materials of which books and documents are made, and this, again, is a blanket description used solely to avoid confusing the issue.

The microbes that adversely affect the materials of books and documents vary very widely in their requirements for nutriment, moisture, temperature and acidity or alkalinity. The basic division of the materials into protein or polysaccharide (pastes, cellulose, etc.) governs to a great extent the type of organism that can be expected to be present and growing, but the presence of glue size on paper and of paste on vellum generally means that any microbe may be found anywhere.

Microbes need moisture and it is commonly assumed that they will not grow when the relative humidity of the atmosphere in equilibrium with the material is below 65 per cent, but while this is a very safe assumption for the practical business of book and document storage it is not an absolute certainty and there is always a possibility, however slight, that a microbe may be found growing when it should not be.

As a general rule, the greater the humidity, the more lush is the microbial growth, but it is probable that the (still unidentified) organism which causes foxing (very probably *Aspergillus Terreus var. aureus,* though other species may also be involved) grows only in a limited and, as far as microbes are concerned, comparatively low range of relative humidity. The ability of both cellulose and collagen to retain tenaciously moisture absorbed from an atmosphere of high relative humidity allows microbes to grow inside a damp book, and some microbes are able to utilize the moisture they generate by degrading cellulose.

Again, as a rough general rule, fungi prefer to grow in acidic conditions and many bacteria prefer neutral or faintly alkaline conditions. It is quite possible that this may to some extent govern which organisms can grow on acid or alkaline paper. Temperature will to some extent govern the rate of microbial growth. Coldness certainly slows down growth, but a temperature over a certain level will inhibit growth, particularly if it causes dehydration. Heat alone, or heat and moisture, are frequently used for the sterilization of surgical instruments, but it must be made absolutely clear that such treatment is far too drastic for use on books or documents, for it damages the cellulose. (For example, a well-baked telephone directory is much easier to tear in half than an unbaked one.)

It is, perhaps, helpful to think of microbial growth as being a rather shadowy area in which there are no sharp distinctions, but rather gradual changes in the ability of the microbe to grow profusely; this applies not only to natural environmental conditions but also to the reactions of the microbe to chemical poisons.

Biocides should be regarded as a last resort in the battle with microbes and one of the purposes of this book is to help the owner or custodian to arrange matters so that they are unnecessary. It is possible, by climatic control alone, to obtain an environment in which microbial growth is, for all practical purposes, absent, but this happy state of affairs will be created only when correct climatic conditions exist in every single part of the store. When microbial infestation does occur, or when infected material has to be taken into a store, the use of chemical fungicides is unavoidable and this is in a large measure due to the fact that the microbes are deeply embedded in the materials of which the books and documents are made, possibly in a dormant sporular form.

The fact that biocides are chemically reactive compounds, whether they and their reaction products are harmful to books and documents or not, makes it necessary to balance the killing efficiency of the biocide against the undesirable effects on the materials in the collection. The wisely cautious policy adopted by archivists and conservators in this country has meant that in practice the comparatively weak fungicide thymol is the one most extensively used. It has a very low toxicity (it is used in throat pastilles), but a very few people may be adversely effected by it. Large record offices use it as a vaporised fumigant, but for the owner or custodian of small collections it is best used as an impregnated tissue interleaved into books or between documents which are being affected by foxing. Its main defect is its ability to dissolve in, plasticise, and make sticky many of the modern synthetic resin adhesives used in bookbinding and some of the inks used in lithography, so a little caution may be required.

A much more powerful fungicide used extensively in the conservation work on the millions of books and documents damaged in the Florentine flood of 1966 is orthophenyl phenol. It is not so readily available to the layman as thymol and it is not volatile enough to be used as a fumigant, but it is a very poor solvent so that it is less likely to affect inks. The preparation and use of fungicidal tissue is described in an appendix.

There are many proprietary disinfectants on the market and these are often a mixture of primary biocide, such as parachlor-meta-xylenol, together with soaps, solvents and other pleasant-smelling compounds. Such materials should never be used directly on books or documents, but there is no reason why they should not be used, in the proportions recommended by the manufacturer, for cleaning shelves and fittings before books are placed on them or during cleaning, provided great care is taken to see that no residues are left on the surface where books will be.

It is possible to dry out books which have become very wet, whether they are mouldy or not, but care is needed and it may be more convenient to put them in strong polythene bags which are closed securely and kept in a deep-freeze. Freezing will arrest damage and halt the growth of fungi, though it does not kill them, until expert care is available.

Biocides should never be used directly on books or documents.

Chemical enemies

The man in the street probably thinks of chemicals as being rather nasty things in bottles, but in truth every solid, liquid or gaseous object in this universe is a chemical or a mixture of chemicals, and this means that both books (and documents) and ourselves are chemicals and can react adversely with other chemicals.

The group of chemicals that is generally reckoned to be the most hazardous to books and documents is the acids, particularly those which the chemist calls 'strong' acids. (The chemist uses the terms 'strong' or 'weak' to describe the power of the individual acid and 'concentrated' or 'dilute' to describe the proportion so present in a solution.) Though concentrated strong acids in general are never found as such in respectable book and document stores, one of them, sulphuric acid, will almost certainly be present in an unobtrusive form and acting surreptitiously. It is present in town air, particularly in industrial cities, and comes from the combustion of sulphur compounds which are present in coal, coke, petrol, oil fuels, and so on. These burn to form a gas, sulphur dioxide, which slowly reacts with more air to form sulphur trioxide, which, in turn, reacts with moisture to form sulphuric acid. The sulphur dioxide and the sulphuric acid can both cling to surfaces and both are very strongly absorbed by lignin from wood, especially in mechanical wood-pulp paper. This is one of the reasons why books made from such paper have a pronounced brown border to the pages: this area of the paper is much more acid, and weaker, than the centre part of the page near the spine of the book.

Alum, used in paper-making, reacts as though it were a weaker form of sulphuric acid. Acids attack cellulose and break the long cellulose molecules into shorter lengths. The cumulative effect on a fibre of having an increasing number of the cellulose molecules broken down is that the fibre as a whole is weakened and thus also the paper of which it forms a part.

Skin, such as parchment and vellum, is also attacked, but as both these materials are impregnated with chalk there is no cause for serious worry and oddly enough, whittawed pigskin, which contains alum, is quite acid and is remarkably durable. Leather, that is, skin which has been treated with a vegetable tanning agent, is much more susceptible to acid attack than is skin, but the effect depends very much on which tan has been used. There is a great deal yet to be learnt about what is really happening.

It has been discovered in recent years that there are other undesirable compounds, particularly oxides of nitrogen and ozone, which act as powerful oxidising agents, and are present in polluted atmospheres. Though their role in damaging books and documents has yet to be assessed, there can be little doubt that they do play some part.

The conservation treatment of acidity in books and documents is not always an easy matter for the expert, let alone the layman, and this is to a large extent due to practical problems. The bibliography at the end of the book will contain the names of some standard works which may be helpful.

Light is an enemy of books and its mode of action is chemical in nature. The extent of the chemical action of light is dependent on the frequency of the light. For any form of radiation, which includes light, Frequency × Wavelength = Velocity of light, which is constant, so the energy of light increases as the wavelength decreases. Ultra-violet light has a wavelength shorter than visible light and so it is more active, that is more destructive to paper and ink. It is usual to screen out ultra-violet light from showcases, but it must be remembered that all light is chemically

Light is an enemy of books . . .

active and it is good conservation practice to display or store books in rooms and cases with a very low level of incident light.

The most noticeable effect of light is the fading of colours, especially of inks and the bindings of books, though this is almost always accompanied by damage to the paper or leather which is less obvious. However, since documents exist to be used, or to be seen for pleasure, loss of only some visual appearance is damage enough, especially as there is no practical remedy.

Heat can also be an enemy of books, for two main reasons. Firstly, it increases the rate at which chemicals, such as acids, attack paper and it is known that books kept in hot places will last for a shorter time than those in cool places. The second reason is that heat, by causing a lowering of

Heat can also be an enemy . . .

relative humidity, produces dimensional changes in materials such as paper, parchment, wood and glue, the basic materials of books and documents. The moisture in cellulose, parchment and glue, which is held by semi-chemical bonds, depends on the relative humidity of the air surrounding them and, therefore, if this air is dried by raising its temperature, the moisture in the materials will be lost and they will contract. This is what causes the bowing of the covers of books read by the fire. The contraction in parchment, vellum and glue can be even more drastic, causing cockling of the leaves and the loss of ink and deocration, and excessive strain on the binding structure.

Another consequence of undue heating is that it will cause moisture to migrate from a warm place to a cooler one. This effect can be seen in any poorly ventilated space, such as a picture frame, a metal deed-box, or a whole room. The increase in moisture at the relatively cool place may often be enough to allow microbes to grow or even to cause staining by liquid water and rust. Furthermore, it is a property of glass that the ease with which it allows radiant heat to pass through it depends on the temperature of the source of that heat. Therefore, heat from the sun can pass through a window and heat a room and the books within it, which is why a greenhouse is hot on a cold sunny day. However, compared with a brick wall a window is a good conductor of heat; since it cannot absorb the heat it is transmitting, it will be cold on a cold day, so that moisture driven out of the books will condense on the window. Air in contact with the window is cooled and drops down the wall space below it, bathing it in a stream of a cold damp air.

Thus, indirectly, windows are an enemy of books, for they allow sunlight to fall on the books so that the ultra-violet light and radiant heat can cause chemical and physical damage to them while at the same time acting as a source of dampness.

Fire and flood are obviously major enemies of books and documents,

There is no ideal fire-extinguisher . . .

and in the minds of librarians and archivists they are regarded as a very closely linked pair, for even a very small fire may result in a major flood damage from the water used to quench it, and this includes damage from the contact of the water jets on the books.

There is no ideal type of fire extinguisher for use on books. Foam or dry powder devices will make a horrid mess and the pressurised water types will wet the books and cause damage. The carbon dioxide gas types are not really effective on burning books and it not entirely safe to use them or the 'BCF' type in a confined space. However, the simple fact is that the quicker a fire is attacked by *any* means, the less the damage from all sources and a fire is most easily quenched in its first half minute.

Local Fire Brigades willingly give advice on the best equipment to use in a given set of circumstances and on its most effective use.

Loss and theft

It can be argued that the prevention of the theft of books is a form of conservation. There is no need to expand on this theme or to do more than to tell the owners and custodians of books that every police force has Crime Prevention Officers who will gladly visit premises and give sensible practical advice.

3

What to do

Having considered the materials of which books and documents may be made and what their enemies may be, it is possible to describe good storage conditions, based on an understanding of these factors, so that the attacks of the various enemies are reduced to the minimum possible. It would be foolish to deny that cost is a major factor in the storage of books and documents and quite often they have to be stored in a way that is known to be undesirable, solely because more space and better shelving would be too expensive. As has been said earlier, the purpose of this booklet is to indicate not merely the ideals at which to aim but the reasons why these ideals exist so that those responsible can plan their resources to obtain the best results and increase the quality of the storgage as more funds become available.

The building

The first consideration must always be the soundness of the building and the room itself, for it is of little use to spend money on any fittings if the floor is too weak to take the weight of the books or the roof can fall in on them. The building must be usable for the purpose, being strong, clean and defensible against fire, flood, theft and vermin. The roof must be sound and free from leaks. The rain that falls on the building must not enter it, so all gulleys and down-pipes must be sound and in working in order. It will be an advantage if they are easily accessible for cleaning.

Damp courses should be sound all round the building and the footings of the external walls must be kept clean from overgrowing weeds and bushes.

The supplies of gas, water and electricity must all be in good order. Water pipes, whether of supply or waste, should not pass through a room in which books may be stored, especially not over the books themselves, or run in such a way that if they do leak, water can fall onto books. Bad electrical wiring may cause fires, particularly if water reaches it.

It goes without saying that the structural wood-work of the building must be sound and free from any form of insect infestation or rot, whether dry or wet, and the same considerations apply to all the other wood-work – windows and their frames, doors and their frames, laths in plaster and ceilings.

External wood-work, such as windows, must be well fitting and effectively painted, the glass being free from cracks. The use of wired glass, or of wire over the glass, should be considered if there is a risk of breakage by vandals.

The author, drawn from life
while giving a lecture.

The store-room

The room itself should not be a basement unless it is known *for certain* that water can never enter it; a ground-floor or first-floor room is better. The floor must be strong enough to carry a heavy load (librarians suggest a figure of 350lb per square foot (158kg per 30 square centimetres)) for a shelf a yard or a metre long may carry 60lb (27kg) of books. If there are windows, the smaller these are the better and they should be capable of being fitted with blinds or thick curtains to exclude sunlight.

The racks of shelving should rest on bases which help to distribute the weight they bear and should run at right angles to the joists. If possible, the racks should be placed away from the walls; if, because of the need to carry the load more safely they have to be placed along the walls, there should be a space of not less than six inches (15cm), preferably a foot (30cm), between the backs of the books or documents so as to allow air to circulate freely. The bottom shelf should be at least six inches (15cm) from the floor, certainly high enough to allow a broom to reach under it easily. If island shelves are to be used, with back-to-back shelving, the division between the two racks should not be solid, but open wire or plastic mesh. Here, too, a gap for air to circulate up and down as well as from side to side would be helpful. When steel racking is used 'end-to-end', it is wise to have a wire or plastic grid or steel plate between the ends of the sections so that air can more easily move between them, in addition to that referred to above with back-to-back shelving.

The spaces between the racks should be enough for users to move easily between them to read titles and to reach and remove any book or box without undue trouble. It is also wise to leave the positioning of the lights until the locations of the racks have been determined. If electric points are fitted, they should be so placed as to allow vacuum cleaners or table lamps to be used easily and safely along the racks.

The racks of shelving may be of metal or of wood. Metal is not liable to insect attack but it is a good conductor of heat, and in order to avoid the risk of condensation it is wise to ensure that no book actually touches metal. A layer of hard board, or of the old-fashioned unglazed cork

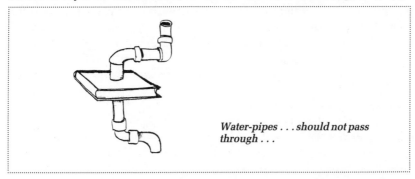

Water-pipes . . . should not pass through . . .

linoleum, can be placed on the bare metal surface; vinyl materials should not be used, for these always contain plasticisers which can bleed out and stain or adhere to book covers. While it is true that wood can be invaded by wood-worms which can pass into the books, wood does not heat up or cool down rapidly and unpainted wood helps to stabilize the relative humidity in the room.

There are several varieties of adjustable shelving and racking available in Do-It-Yourself shops, and the private owner who does not want to use the traditional glass-fronted cases can choose what he likes to suit his needs on the basis of the advice given above.

The climate in the room

It is essential that air should be able to circulate freely round and through the stacks. Provided that this is possible, it is not really important for heating apparatus to be installed. It may well be that the store is better without it, for as has been said earlier, heat alone can be of no service to a book or document and is more likely than not to be deleterious. If the room is purely a store and someone has to work in it only intermittently, a small radiant type electric fire can be used, so placed as to direct its heat only on the worker and not on the books. It is only the user who needs warmth.

If high humidity is a problem even when all building faults have been corrected, because of the naturally high relative humidity of the district, the action to be taken will depend on several factors. If the collection concerned is small and kept in a lived-in room, part of a family home, then it should, so to speak, have family home treatment in that it would be kept dry as that room would be, by artificial heating and ventilation, particular attention being paid to the need for air to circulate freely round the books, so an open case is safer than a closed one.

If the room is purely a store for books and documents, there is no virtue at all in heating the room solely in an attempt to dry it safely, and the best course is to use a de-humidifier. These draw in air, cool it to condense the moisture out and then re-warm the air, the water being discharged. These are not necessarily cheap but the running costs are remarkably low and they can be set to run on a time switch or on a humidity switch. The advantages are that the moisture is not pumped to the cold parts of the room but collected, and the forced circulation of the air ensures that a much larger area of the room is controlled effectively. De-humidifiers cannot, of course, rapidly draw moisture from the inside of a damp book or box of damp documents and if an excessively damp room is being brought under control it may well be necessary to have the books opened fanwise and document boxes opened.

Quite often, what the housewife would call 'a good airing' will improve the climate in a book and document store, the windows being opened on a fine, dry, breezy day even a bitterly cold one. It is often helpful to use oscillating fans to circulate air or to have an exhaust fan set into a panel closing off a fireplace. These need be used only for the odd hour or two in a week but whether they are refinements or necessities will be governed by circumstances.

Excessive dryness in any part of the British Isles is no fault of our climate and is almost invariably due to excessive heating. It cannot be too strongly stressed that high temperatures are harmful, not only in their own right but also becuase they lower the relative humidity. Attempts to raise the relative humidity artificially do not prevent the primary damage and may well accelerate it, apart from increasing the risk of microbial growth. The simple answer to the problem is to reduce the heating by any available means. The heat in sunlight can be reduced considerably by fitting Venetian blinds or curtains inside windows and radiators can be turned off.

Thermometers and hygrometers

It is wise to have instruments to measure the climatic conditions in a room where books and documents are stored but these need only to be of a simple kind. Alcohol or mercury themometers are generally more reliable than the simple thermocouple dial instrument and a gardener's maximum and minimum thermometer is exceptionally useful, as it reports extremes as well as the ambient temperatures. The thermometers used in photographic processing usually have a short range but widely spaced markings, which makes reading easy.

A wet and dry bulb hygrometer is usually more reliable than a 'hair' or 'paper' dial instrument, provided that it is properly set up, but when cost is a major factor and many places must be monitored it may be necessary to buy several cheap instruments. Small, cheap hygrometers can be checked by suspending them over a saturated solution of a specific salt in water, contained in a closed jar (*see* Appendix 6).

Nevertheless, however many instruments may be bought and installed or how often they are read, the most valuable evidence comes from the books or documents themselves, and there is no substitute for regular visual checks in which the items are examined for the stiffness or limpness of the sheets, musty smell, worm damage, and so on.

It is wise to have instruments . . .

Small collections

Not all people who want to preserve books or documents have large collections; it may be that the collection is quite small, too small to consider a separate room, and a single case only may suffice. Oddly enough, the problems of producing a safe climate in a single case may be more difficult than those for a single room, especially in a centrally-heated flat.

In a clean rural atmosphere, where excessive humidity is not a continual problem, provided that adequate air circulation round the material can be achieved, storage in any room with an equable cool temperature is satisfactory, provided that the other general requirements can be met. Sunlight should not fall on the books, they must not be subject to physical damage, and so on.

In a heavily polluted industrial atmosphere, even in a 'Clean Air Zone' there is little alternative to the use of a closed case. A glass-fronted case can act as a heat-trap and it is more important than ever to ensure that this does not happen. Such a case must be placed where the sun cannot shine on it at any season of the year. A case with wooden doors is better, but it is easy to forget that there are books or documents in it. Whatever sort of case or cupboard is used it is better have it too large rather than too small, with the books clear of the backs and sides.

Provided that the temperature is reasonably steady and changes slowly, a closed case of which the walls, doors, etc. are insulators, for example wood, is an excellent device for controlling the relative humidity, for the special relationship that exists between cellulose and moisture will help to stabilise this. It is very unwise to use a metal case as a store for valuable books unless there is very exact temperature control. Whatever case or cupboard is used, regular inspections and frequent, at least fortnightly, airings are essential. Wood-worm infestation is the main hazard.

The single book . . . is easily cared for . . .

The care of a single book

The single valuable, important or fragile book is easily cared for. It should be wrapped in cotton wool, to form a layer about an inch thick over it, and then placed in a wooden box. The box should be natural wood rather than chipboard or blockboard and left unvarnished. If the book is on parchment or vellum and seen to be over-dry, the cotton wool should be hung up in a cool damp place for a day before being used. After a week or so, the cotton wool should be replaced by freshly humidified material and so on until the book is in a satisfactory condition. It is best to let this happen slowly.

Documents

So far, wherever possible, the phrase 'books and documents' has been used to imply that the matter discussed concerns both bound books and gatherings of documents. Documents can come in all shapes and sizes and are most simply dealt with according to size, in three simple categories:
1. Foolscap (including A4), and sheets from half to twice that size.
2. Large sheets to be kept flat.
3. Large sheets that can be rolled up.

Foolscap and thereabouts

Ordinary papers of this size can be boxed, or made into parcels, or stored as current files are. The boxes which archivists use for indefinitely long storage are normally stouter than commercial box files and are usually made of board of a higher quality, in that it has low acidity and little mechanical wood-pulp. The cheaper alternative is to make a neat parcel of the documents using an acid-free wrapping paper, including acid-free boards to provide rigidity to the parcel, which must be tied with tape, not string.

Small sheets of parchment or vellum require more care than does paper. Folded or crumpled sheets ought to be flattened only by experts. The small sheets are probably best stored between sheets of clean white blotting paper held between sheets of card, tied with tape. These

There is a very simple practice in rolling documents . . .

sandwiches can be kept in boxes or drawers, the usual provisos about temperature, humidity, woodworm, etc. always applying.

Large sheets to be kept flat

Large documents are not to be folded, but if this must be done, two simple rules are to be obeyed: use as few folds as possible; never fold through anything that matters. Having given that important advice, the manner of storing such documents depends on their number and material of which they are made. A few large documents are best kept in a large flat box which a handyman can make from hardboard and deal battens. The box should be lined with good quality drawing paper using acid-free paste. A large number of flat documents are best kept in a wooden plan-chest rather than a metal one.

Large documents on parchment or vellum, if unfolded, can have tissue paper placed either side of them, with an outer layer of blotting paper or clean cotton wool, supported between large sheets of good quality card tied with tapes. The 'sandwiches' can be stored in boxes or wooden plan-chests. If the documents have seals attached, the methods for their handling are described in British Standard 5454: 1978, 'Recommendations for the Storage and Exhibition of Documents'. Again, the proper precautions regarding temperature, humidity, etc. always apply.

Large sheets that can be rolled

There is a very simple practice in rolling documents and its observance distinguishes the professional archivist and conservator from the amateur. The professional rolls documents round the *outside* of a strong cardboard tube which is covered by a protective layer of good quality paper and is longer than the maximum dimension of the document. The document is then covered with an outer protective layer, large enough to have its ends tucked into the ends of the tube. The ideal way of mounting a document to a tube with guards, flaps, etc. is described in the British Standard and in many books on document repair, but the basic requirements can be understood from the description given above.

Repairs to books and documents

It should be clear from what has been written so far that books and documents are complex objects, so it follows that repair work requires knowledge, skill and experience which cannot be learnt solely from books. For these reasons, no mention has been made in this book of methods of repair, but in the bibliography there are the names of textbooks which cover the subject. British Standard 4971: 1973, *Recommendations for the Treatment of Documents* contains excellent advice as to what may or may not be done, together with useful appendices on adhesives, and so on. Many local education authorities now have classes on bookbinding, and any owner or custodian who wishes to undertake his own repair work should join one.

Advice on repair work to books and documents can often be obtained from the local County or City Records Office as almost without exception they have well-trained conservators. The local record office can usually advise on the choice of pest exterminators if an insect or rodent infestation occurs and will have a list, compiled by members of the Society of Archivists, of suppliers and equipment.

4

Summing up

The basis on which the proper storage of books and documents is founded is, quite simply, good housekeeping taken in its fullest extension.

When undertaking the storage of books and documents, it is essential to bear in mind that the owner or custodian may be absent for a long period. If the storage is devised and arranged correctly the material, because of its chemical and physical nature, can play a major role in maintaining correct conditions in its own store.

The main things to consider are as follows:

1. The building must be sound in all respects.
2. The rooms used as a store must be sound in all respects.
3. The room must be easy to keep clean and inspect thoroughly.
4. The free circulation of air is probably the most important single factor in the climatic conditions for the safe storage of books.
5. Every effort should be made to ensure an even climate, changing as slowly as can be managed, throughout the room.
6. The room is better cold than warm.

Right *Two small insect holes in the cover of a book. The larger one is ¾ in (1.9 cm) from one edge, ½ in (1.3 cm) from the other. Inside the book (below), the damage extends through 23 leaves.*

Below *Typical silver-fish and firebrat damage on modern paper. The edges are thinned away rather than bored through. Eighteenth-century pure rag paper in contact with this piece was left untouched.*

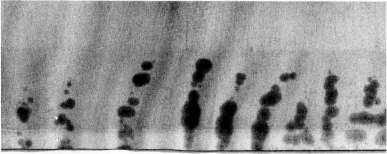

Top *Mildew and some diffuse foxing on paperbacks which were kept against the outside wall of the upstairs room of a dry house.*

Centre *The actual volume of air occupied by the unsafe climate may be very small. In this case it is the air space in a crinkle little more than ⅛ in (0.3 cm) across, ½₀ in (0.13 cm) deep. The longest line of mould growth is just over an inch long. The paper lay against glass.*

Below *A photograph at very high magnification of the fungal growth in the foxing on the spines of the paperbacks.*
Taken in the British Museum Research Laboratory by Mr N. D. Meetis.

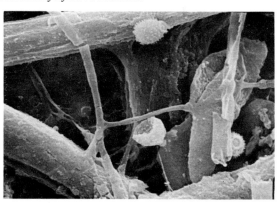

Small entrance holes made by insects (?) visible on the outside of a book (right) lead to large cavities inside (below).

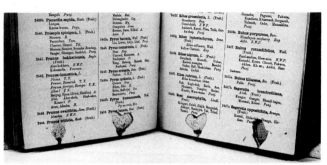

Below left *Really extensive foxing on a print. This is due to a micro-organism which has not yet been identified. Very little is known for certain about it.*

Below right *Foxing on the fore-edge of a book. The relative humidity in the centre of the room was c. 75%. This book was in a case against an inside wall.*

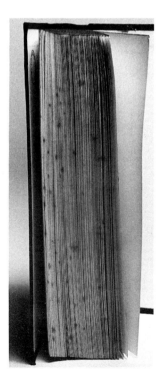

Right *Extensive variegated fungal growth on a well-wetted book (found on a rubbish dump). Bad as it may appear to be, little real damage has been done and the book is usable.*

Below left *Dry rot in a book which became beyond repair and had to be burnt.*

Below right *Water in the upright of this steel shelving from a flood caused sufficient humidity to support mould growth in books touching it; the openings in the shelves are clearly marked on the books.*

Appendices

1 Creating a small book store

After the first edition of this book had been published, the author had the opportunity to buy a well-constructed brick building with some windows and was able to put into practice what he had learnt, and what he had been teaching, in order to house his own collection. The books in this collection ranged in size from 'large', that is, over 11in (28cm) high to small, less than 7in (18cm) high, the majority lying between these limits. It was anticipated that, in due course, they would be indexed on the Decimal System. For practical reasons, the shelf heights had to be adjustable and this dictated the use of racking fitted with 'library strip'. The design of the building made it advisable to have a space of at least 12in (30cm) behind the books, the walls being made of insulating blocks. A space of 12in (30cm) was made between the lowest shelf and the concrete floor, which meant that the top shelf, reserved for large books, was 7ft from the floor, for library strip is made in 6ft lengths.

For those of a practical nature it may be added that the grooves for the library strip were cut with a router, but apart from this, the only tools required were the usual ones of a tenon saw, electric drill, screwdrivers, etc. The racking was assembled on a simple jig and the positions for the screws holding the racking together were marked from a template.

A colleague who kept his collection in his dry house used a wall-mounted bracket system, but fixed the supporting strip to a 2in × 1in (5cm × 2.5cm) batten which was screwed to the wall in order to increase the amount of air space behind the books.

The author has no permanent heating in his library building, but in very cold weather uses a small electric fan heater directed at himself. A small dehumidifier is installed, which is not operated in cold weather because the low temperatures in this unheated building do not allow the moisture frozen out of the air to melt and run away. Before it was used, the only occasion on which very slight fungal growth was observed, on some half-dozen books, was in a warm damp spring after a prolonged cold spell. The books most affected had been heavily fingered and had impervious covers.

2 Inspecting a collection of books and documents

It is essential that those who have charge of a collection should inspect it at regular intervals to make sure that it is in a proper conditon and this inspection should include the relevant parts of the outside and inside of the building. It is useful to make inspections in several different weather conditions, the best being bitter cold, a warm wet spell after cold, pouring rain and during hot weather.

The things to look out for externally are damage such as broken windows, missing roof tiles, damage or faults to guttering, rain water heads and down-pipes, undue wet on walls, algal or lichen growth on walls etc., that is, all the general indications that water is going, or can go, where it should not. Grass should not be growing in gutters, birds should not be nesting in ventilators or rainwater heads.

Inside the building it is important to look for such faults as damp patches on walls, ceilings and floors which can be traced to condensation, a defective damp course, water from defective gutters or down-pipes seeping through from outside, wet patches under windows from rot or other damage in the window frames and leaking from any pipes which may pass through the room.

It is wise to enter the room carefully and to sniff hard to see if the room smells damp. It is a simple but very useful test for, if the room smells clean, it is unlikely to be damp, which is reassuring. Simple mustiness coupled with what can best be described as the smell of old books usually requires no more than airing to remove it, but a real damp smell may indicate a building fault that must be rectified, or the need to use a de-humidifier, even if only on a short-term but regular basis. A good sniff round in all parts of the room, in corners, behind racking, etc. will give you more information.

Those who are of a scientific or technical turn of mind and who care for important collections, be they small or large, especially if they have several in their charge, may like to use a small portable moisture meter to check the moisture contents of walls, woodwork and books.

As far as the books and their cases or racks are concerned, the inspection should be directed towards biological hazards. The presence of insects, dead or alive, should be noted and an effort made to identify them. Some may be harmless, but their very presence indicates that insects can enter. Any fresh or clean 'frass' should be noted and its source determined; it may be old, from old holes left by a dead infestation but it may not be, and in this case the extent of the new infestation must be determined. The presence of moth wings suggests that bats have access, for they eat the bodies alone. A whitish appearance on buckram bindings on low shelves may be mould, but it may be due to the loss of paste that has been eaten by fire-brats or silver fish and the source of that infestation may not be within the room itself. Silver fish prefer to live in dark damp and fire-brats like it warm, such as around underfloor heating pipes. If either are suspected, the characteristic 'contouring' damage to leaves should be searched for; this is more likely to occur in paper made after c.1860.

The presence of mouse droppings, whether of house or field mouse, should be looked for as should chewed-up or shredded paper which suggests that a nest is present. Obviously, bird droppings should be noted too.

It is wise to take books from the shelves in a regular repeating pattern to check for less obvious damage, for some insects may eat the faces of covers of touching books rather than eat the spine. It is also quite easy to miss worm holes on the foredges or bottom edges of books.

Fungi are most likely to be found on the exterior of the books, either as mildew, or worse, on the spines, tops and foredges of books and though it grows only slowly, foxing too may be found on exposed paper. Prolonged damp will lead to foxing inside the book, but it is capricious and some books may be badly affected while others remain untouched. Dryrot should not occur, though it can move into a room through brickwork and floorboards to the shelves and cause devastating damage as it rises up through the books.

If damage is found, it must be dealt with, but even if none is seen, it is wise to sweep the floors, window sills and shelves carefully so that any infestation can more readily be spotted on the next inspection. Careful sweeping and dusting may reveal traces of insects, etc. that might otherwise have been missed.

It cannot be stressed too strongly that careful, conscientious and thoughtful inspection is of the utmost importance in caring for libraries and archives;

observation is one of the foundations of scientific, or any other, discovery, and as the great Hungarian chemist Szent György said: 'Discoveries are made when someone sees what everyone else has seen and thinks what no one else has thought.'

3 Organising a collection

Any collection of books or documents, however small, will cover a range of subjects, and clearly it is helpful for the user to arrange the books in a proper order; the main purpose of such a collection is that any item in it can be located quickly when it is wanted for use, and 'use' includes a study of the text, bibliographical study and, of course, pleasure. Apart from this, when books and documents are always in known, definite places, it is easier to check not only that they are present, but to notice any damage arising.

Those who own or care for such a collection may therefore wish to index the material. The indexing of archival and other documents is a specialised matter and those who wish to do it are advised to approach an archivist (every large local authority has one), a map librarian, music librarian or similar specialist. For books, BS 1000, 'Universal Decimal Classification', covers the whole field in great, sometimes almost daunting, but always practical detail. The user should remember, though, that the system is his servant, not his master, and that he can be as flexible as he chooses in assigning numbers to his own books for his own purposes, neither need he be over precise. The aim need only be to get into reasonably close proximity books which he regards as belonging together, and for this reason it is probably not necessary to use the most up-to-date or comprehensive part of the Standard.

There are certain overriding conditions, mentioned earlier in this book, referring to the safest way to store books on shelves. Physically, books come into three simple classes, large, medium and small and, as has been said earlier, it is wise to put books of the same size together and to put together those books which require special care.

Books can also be divided by subject, for example fiction, biography, non-fiction. Apart from these categories, it is pleasant to set aside in one place what are called 'association books', school and college prizes, treasured presents, etc., and useful to put essential reference books together. As a variant, the uniform size and wide range of subjects in a series such as 'Everyman's Library' makes it convenient to keep these together. Paperbacks are mostly of uniform size and, again, it is often convenient to keep them together.

4 Electronic records

The increasing use of computers and word-processors makes it more than likely that their products will find their way into collections and have to be cared for. There are several classes of these computer products, such as text-on-paper (print-out), punched paper tapes, magnetic tapes, floppy discs, compact discs, etc., and there is every reason to believe that the number will increase. It has to be understood from the beginning that, save for text-on-paper, none of it resembles the material that has for the last three millennia accumulated in libraries and archives in that the text that it carries can only be read by a particular machine read in a particular way, which must be known and available to the would-be reader.

It is essential therefore that every item of such material received into a collection must be labelled clearly and permanently not only with its identity but with the means by which it was produced and can be reread. It is the practice in libraries and archives that an annual review is made to ensure that compatible 'readers' still exist. Further, since the 'text' is recorded magnetically, a check is made for 'print through' on tapes which are to be stored for long periods and it is usual to rewind the tape end-to-end to avoid this problem. (This is also a wise precaution with little-used audio tapes, especially those on long tapes.) It has to be remembered that with the rapid developments and changes in computers, if compatible readers are not available, the material is useless.

It is unfortunate, also, that paper and ink of print-out text from computers is almost invariably of poor quality; both are liable to rapid decay, especially in light.

Notwithstanding these problems, the general rules for the storage of computer products are similar to those for ordinary text, save that since the 'text' is often produced magnetically, it is sensitive to magnetic fields, a matter which does not concern the keepers of traditional materials. Magnetic fields are produced by electrical equipment such as electric motors, dynamos, generators, central heating controls and lightning conductors, so conditions for care may extend beyond the room in which the material is stored.

The general rules then are:

1 All print-out must be stored in closed boxes, preferably of archival quality.

2 All magnetically produced material must be stored away from electrical equipment that can generate magnetic fields.

3 All tapes, discs, etc. must be kept in boxes and handled with the same care as books.

4 All material which is not directly visually readable must be clearly and permanently labelled with the means by which it was produced and by which it can be read.

5 The climatic conditions for the care of computer products can be taken as being similar to those required for conventional reading matter.

6 It cannot be assumed that computer products will not be liable to biodeterioration. It has been reported that mice will eat floppy discs! Material into which mould growth has spread will, at the very least, be unpleasant to handle and possibly difficult to 'read' without expert cleaning.

Sound recordings should be stored in clean dry conditions so that they cannot distort and dust cannot reach them. Fungi can readily attack the record sleeves and grow over, if not live on, the discs themselves. If this fungal attack occurs, very careful cleaning, usually by washing, is required and the only check that damage has not occurred, or that cleaning has been effective, is for the disc to be played on good equipment, while being listened to by someone with perfect pitch.

5 Making fungicidal tissue

The difficulty that arises in making fungicidal tissue is that as the solution used is alkaline, the tissue becomes very floppy and weak. There are various tricks which will help. One way is to lay a large sheet of polythene, such as an opened-out dustbin liner on a table, lay sheets of tissue on it, paint them with the solution and leave them to dry. If the tissue is not made too wet, it will cling to the polythene, which can be hung on a line to dry, tissue and all.

The solution used is alkaline, rather like strong washing soda, so it is important to wear rubber gloves and to avoid splashing it onto the face, food, furniture, the cat and so on. The chemist's rule is that if he gets a chemical splashed in his eye, he sees a doctor. This particular chemical is not regarded as poisonous but it requires respect.

Method

Make up a solution containing about 5 per cent weight/volume of sodium orthophenyl phenate in water, by adding one ounce of the solid to one pint of water (25g to half a litre of water). Paint this solution onto a strong tissue, such as is used for wrapping silver. Soft toiletry tissues are too weak for this purpose.

Allow the tissue to dry thoroughly before using it, storing it if need be in a polythene bag. Spare solution should be kept in a plastic bottle and labelled 'Sodium orthophenyl phenate 5%. Not to be taken', preferably in red, and should be kept out of reach of children.

Use

Place a leaf of tissue, a little smaller than the page, every eighth of an inch (3mm) in the book. This will increase the bulk of the book, so do *not* force it shut. If it will not fit easily back into its place on the shelf, put it in a clean, dry plastic bag and leave it for a month, at least, before removing the tissue.

6 Checking hygrometers

When certain salts are dissolved in water, with an excess of solid present, and kept in a closed container with air, the air will have a known constant relative humidity. If there is doubt as to the reliability of the reading of a hygrometer, it is possible to use this fact to check the instrument. The closed container could be a Kilner Jar (the modern variety with a metal lid) with the instrument suspended over about an inch (2.5cm) or so of the saturated solution and left there for a day to settle to a steady reading.
Three salts suitable for this purpose are:

Potassium carbonate – relative humidity 43%
Use two ounces (50g) of the solid to one fluid ounce (30ml) of cold water

Magnesium acetate – relative humidity 65%
Add a little cold water to the solid to make a slurry. This substance can dissolve in less than its own weight of water
Ammonium chloride – relative humidity 80%
Use one ounce (25g) of the solid to two fluid ounces (60ml) of cold water

These materials are non-toxic and should be available by order through a pharmacist. However, as with all chemicals, treat them with respect, label the containers clearly, and keep them out of the reach of children.

Bookshelf

Allsopp, D. and Seal, K. J., *Introduction to Biodeterioration,* Edward Arnold (Pub) Ltd., 41 Bedford Square, WC1B 3DQ, 1986 (620.1122)

Baker, John and Soroka, Marguerite C., comp., *Library Conservation. Preservation in Perspective,* Dowden Hutchinson & Ross Inc., Stroudsburg, Pennsylvania, 1978 (010)

Browning, B. L., *Analysis of Paper,* Marcel Dekker Inc., New York, 1969 (676.3)

Burdett, Eric, *The Craft of Bookbinding,* David and Charles, Newton Abbot, Devon. 1st Ed. 1975, 2nd imp. 1978 (655.72)

Busvine, J. R., *Insects and Hygiene,* 2nd Ed., Methuen, London, 1966, 3rd Ed., paperback, Chapman and Hall, 1980 (595.7)

Carter, H., *A View of Early Typography,* Clarendon Press, 1969 (655.1)

Carter, J., *An ABC for Book Collectors,* 5th Ed., Hart Davis, London, 1972 (010)

Clair, C., *A Chronology of Printing,* Cassell, 1969 (010)

Clements, J., *Bookbinding,* Arco, London, 1963 (655.72)

Cockerell, D., *Bookbinding and the Care of Books,* Pitman, London, 1963 (686)

Cockerell, S. M., *The Repairing of Books,* Sheppard, London, 1958 (025.7)

Collison, R. L., *Commercial and Industrial Records Storage,* Benn, London, 1969 (651.5)

Corderoy, J. S., *Bookbinding for Beginners,* Studio Vista, London, 1967 (655.7)

Crane, Walter, *The Decorative Illustration of Books,* Geo. Bell & Sons Ltd., 9 Portugal St., W.C.2, re-issued 1972 (741)

Cunha, G. M. and Cunha, D. G., *Library and Archives Conservation: 1980s and beyond,* 2 Vols, Scarecrow Press, Metucken, N.J., 1983 (025.8)

Cunha, G. D. M., *Conservation of Library Materials,* Scarecrow, Metuchen, N.J., 1967 (025.8)

Darley, L. S., *Introduction to Bookbinding,* Faber and Faber, London, 1965 (655.72)

Diehl, Edith, *Bookbinding, Its Background and Technique,* 2 Vols in one, Dover Publications Inc., 180 Varich Street, New York, 10014. Originally published by Rinehart, 1946 (655.72)

Febvre, L. and Martin, H-J, *The Coming of the Book (The Impact of Printing, 1450–1800),* Editions Albin Michel 1985, NLB 1976, 2nd imp. 1979 (655.1)

Flieder, Mme F., *La Conservation des Documents Graphiques, Recherches Experimentales,* Eyrolles, Paris, 1969 (025.7)

Flyate, D. M., (Ed.) *Preservation of Documents and Papers,* I.P.S.T. Jerusalem, H. A. Humphrey Ltd., London, 1968 (025.8)

Grant, J., *Laboratory Handbook of Pulp and Paper Manufacture,* Edward Arnold, London, 1960 (676)

Grant, J., *Cellulose Pulp,* Leonard Hill, London, 1958 (676)

Griffiths, A., *Prints and Printmaking,* BM Publications Ltd., 1980 (741)

Harrison, W. R., *Suspect Documents,* 2nd Impression, with Supplement, Sweet and Maxwell, London, 1958 and 1966 (364.12)

Hector, L. C., *The Handwriting of English Documents,* Edward Arnold, London, 1958 (417)

Hickin, Norman, *Bookworms. The Insect Pests of Books,* Sheppard Press, London, 1985 (595.7)

Hickin, Norman, *Pest Animals in Buildings. A World Review* George Godwin, London 1985 (595.7)

Hind, A. M., *A History of Engraving and Etching*, Dover Publications Inc., New York, 1963 (741)

Horton, C., *Cleaning and Preserving Bindings and Related Material*, A.L.A. Technology Program, Chicago, 1967, 1969 (025.7)

Hunter, D., *Paper Making*, Borzoi Books, Knopf, New York, 2nd edition, 1967 (676)

ICOM Collection, *Problems of Conservation in Museums*, Eyrolles, Paris, 1969 (069.4)

Iiams, Thos. H. and Beckworth, T. D., *Notes on the Causes and Prevention of Foxing in Books*, H. W. Edwards, 4 Cecil Court, WC2, 1937 (025.171)

Jenkinson, Sir H., *Manual of Archive Administration*, Lund Humphries, London, 1966 (022)

Johnson, A. W., *The Thames and Hudson Manual of Bookbinding*, Thames and Hudson, London, 1978 (655.72)

Le Gear, C. E., *Maps. Their Care, Repair and Preservation in Libraries*, Map Division Reference Department, Library of Congress, Washington D.C., 1956 (025.176)

Levey, M., *Medieval Arabic Bookmaking and its relation to early Chemistry and Pharmacology*, Transactions of the American Philosophical Society, New Series, Volume 52, Part 4, 1962. American Philosophical Society, Independence Square, Philadelphia 6 (667.4)

Lewis, Naphtali, *Papyrus in Classical Antiquity*, Oxford, Clarendon Press, 1974 (676)

Library Association Publication, *The Care of Books and Documents*, Library Association, London, 1972 (025.8)

Metcalf, K. D., *Planning Academic and Research Libraries*, McGraw-Hill, New York, 1965 (022)

Middleton, B. C., *The Restoration of Leather Bookbindings*, ALA Tech. Program, Chicago, 1972 (025.7)

Middleton, B. C., *History of English Craft Bookbinding Technique*, Hafner, New York, 1963 (655.72)

Morison, S., *On Type Designs Past and Present*, Benn, 1962 (655.1)

Mourier, H. and Winding, O., *Collins Guide to Wildlife in House and Home*, Collins, London, 1977 (G. E. C. Gadd, Copenhagen, 1975) (502)

National Fire Protection Association, *Protection of Records*, Leaflet 232, NFPA, Boston, Mass., 1970 (069.4)

National Fire Protection Association, *Protection of Museum Collections*, Leaflet 911, Boston, Mass., (069.4)

National Fire Protection Association, *Protection of Library Collections*, Leaflet 910, NFPA, Boston, Mass., 1970 (069.4)

Nielsen, Ingelise, *Papyrus. Structure, Manufacture and Deterioration*, Konservatorskolen, Copenhagen, 1985 (676)

Norris, F. H., *The Nature of Paper and Board*, Pitman, London, 1966 (676.3)

Osborn, A. S., *Questioned Documents*, Boyd Printing Co., Albany, N.Y., 2nd Ed., 1929 (364.12)

Petrova, L. G., Belyakova, L. A. and Kosulina, O. V., Eds, *Collection of Materials on the Preservation of Library Resources. – Title Page, Restoration and Preservation of Library Resources, Documents and Books*, IPST Jerusalem, Oldborne Press, London, 1964 (025.8)

Plenderleith, H. J., *Preservation of Documentary Material in the Pacific Area*, (Australian Nat. Advisory Committee for UNESCO) Australian Govt. Publishing Service, 1972 (025.7)

Plenderleith, H. J. and Werner, A. E., *The Conservation of Antiquities and Works of Art,* OUP, 1972 (069.4)

Plovgaard, S., *Public Library Buildings,* English Translation of Folkebiblioteks-bygningen, Danish State Library Inspectorate, 1967, Library Association, London, 1971 (022)

Reed, R., *Ancient Skins, Leathers and Parchments,* Seminar Press, 1972 (745.3)

Rhodes, H. T. F., *The Craft of Forgery,* John Murray, London, 1934 (364.12)

Robinson, I., *Introducing Bookbinding,* Batsford, 1968 (655.7)

Rose, A. H., (Ed) *Microbial Biodeterioration,* Academic Press, London, 1981 (620.1122)

Shorter, A. H., *Papermaking in the British Isles,* David and Charles, 1963 (338.476762)

Smith, G., *Introduction to Industrial Mycology,* 7th Ed., edited by A. N. S. Onions, D. Allsopp and H. O. W. Eggins, Edward Arnold, 1981 (660.62)

Steinberg, S. H., *Five Hundred Years of Printing,* Penguin, 1974, Faber & Faber, 1959 (655.1)

Studley, V., *The Art and Craft of Handmade Paper,* Studio Vista, London, 1978 (676)

Thomson, R. G. H., *The Museum Environment,* Butterworth, London, 1978, 2nd Ed., 1986 (025.7)

Town, L., *Bookbinding by Hand,* Faber & Faber, London, 2nd ed., 1963 (655.7)

Turner, S., and Skiöld, Birgit, *Handmade Paper Today,* Lund Humphries, London, 1983 (676)

(No author given), *Papermaking Fibres,* Tullis Russell & Co., Markinch, Fife, 1950 (676)

UNESCO/Australia, *The Conservation of cultural materials in Humid Climates,* Australian Government Publishing Service, Canberra, 1980 (028)

Valentine, Lucia M., *Ornament in Medieval Manuscripts,* Faber, 1965 (096)

Vaughan, A. J., *Modern Bookbinding,* Charles Shilton, 1960 (655.7)

Wächter, Otto, *Restaurierung und Erhaltung von Büchern, Archivalien und Graphiken,* Herman Böhlaus, Wien, 1982 (655.72)

Wächter, Wolfgang, *Buchrestaurierung,* VEB Fachverlag, Leipsig, 1983, 2 Auflage (655.72)

Wardle, D. B., *Document Repair,* Soc. of Archivists, London, 1971 (025.7)

Watrous, J. A., *The Craft of Old Master Drawings,* Univ. of Wisconsin Press, 1957 (741)

Williams, John C. (Editor), *Preservation of Paper and Testiles of Historic and Artistic Value,* American Chemical Society, Washington, D.C., 1977, Advances in Chemistry Series, No.164 (686)

Williams, John C. (Editor), *Preservation of Paper and Textiles of Historic and Artistic Value,* Pt. 2, American Chemical Society, Washington, D.C., 1981, Advances in Chemistry No 193 (686)

Wilson, W. K. and Gear, J. L., *Care of Documents, Prints and Films,* A Consumers' Guide from the National Bureau of Standards, Superintendent of Documents, US Government Printing Office, Washington, D.C., Dec. 1971 (025.7)

Winger, H. W. and Smith, R. D., *Deterioration and Preservation of Library Materials,* University of Chicago, 1970 (025.7)

Zerdoun Bat-Yehouda, M., *Les encres noires au Moyen Age (jusqu'a 1600),* CNRS Paris, 1983, Editions du Centre National de la Recherche Scientifique, 15 Quai Anatole France 75700 Paris (667.4)